THE LIVE-IN CARER'S HANDBOOK

A nitty-gritty guide to working as a live-in carer in the UK (and elsewhere)

FIONA SMITH

With a special chapter on tax by GERDA FOUCHÉ

First Published 2024 by Fiona Smith
Copyright © 2024 Fiona Smith

ISBN 978-1-0672378-2-0 (Print)
ISBN 978-1-0672378-1-3 (eBook)

Cover and interior crafted with love by the team at
www.myebook.online

All rights reserved.
No part of this publication may be reproduced, distributed or transmitted
in any form or by any means, including photocopying, recording, or other
electronic or mechanical methods, without the prior written permission of
the publisher, except in the case of brief quotations embodied in critical
reviews and certain other noncommercial uses permitted by copyright law.

*This handbook is dedicated to care
workers all over the world.*

CONTENTS

Introduction

1. The Basics Of Live-In Care   1

2. A Word On The Money   7

3. Realities Of Live-In Care   11

4. A State Of Independence   13

5. Planning And Preparation   17

6. The Interview   25

7. Getting Set Up In The UK   29

8. What Care Workers Say About Live-In Care   33

9. Ten Lessons For Live-In Care   39

10. Interfering vs Caring – it's all about perception   51

11. Arrivals and Departures   53

12. Before I Forget... Dementia Care   57

13. Taxing Times   65

14. One Last Thing...a note on dying   69

15. Conclusion   73

Acknowledgements   76

Useful Links And References   77

Recommended Reading   78

About the Author   79

Author's Note   80

INTRODUCTION

---

*'Never believe that a few caring people can't
change the world. For, indeed, that's all who
ever did.'* **- Margaret Mead**

When I was contemplating coming to the UK to work as a live-in carer, there was no book I could read to explain what live-in care was all about. I asked a few people who were doing caring in the UK, and their responses were: *'You care for the person in the comfort of their own home, the money's good, the hours are long, but you get to choose when you work and for how long. You'll learn new skills. It is extremely rewarding knowing you are helping someone stay in their own home.'*

Many of the live-in care workers in the UK come from different countries and for many varied reasons. Some are escaping financial hardship, others emotional trauma, but there are those who are doing it simply for the experience of living and working in another country. Some consider caring to be a selfless, noble profession. Some are naturally drawn to it and see it as their calling. There are others who relegate it to the lowly rung of a menial job, and then there are the ones who exclaim: *'I could never do that!'* Be that as it may, millions of people all over the world rely on someone else to take care of them, and caring has become an enormously profitable industry. In the UK alone, there are more than 12500 registered home care providers offering care to the elderly, the infirm, and those who are unable to care for themselves for whatever reason. It has become specialised, with Dementia care, Stroke care, Palliative care, and Disability care demanding more qualified carers.

Many training facilities have emerged, yet the shortage of care workers in the industry is creating great concern. Brexit cut off easy access to a much-needed workforce from the

EU, and the Covid 19 lockdown has also had devastating effects on the industry. Thousands of people were removed from hospitals and placed in over-burdened care homes, instead of being sent home and cared for there. The death toll was enormous. This highlighted the need for a radical change in social care, and the concept of *live-in care (people being cared for in their own homes)*, also referred to as *home care*, is being more widely recognized in the industry as an alternative to residential care homes. Live-in care is a person-centred approach where the well-being of the client always comes first.

My intention for writing this handbook is to offer sound, practical advice about working as a live-in carer. It is directed at those wanting to work in the UK, but the tenets of good caring can be applied anywhere in the world. When I looked online for advice and information on *live-in care* from *the care worker's perspective*, I did not find much. Most of the information about live-in care is directed at the client: what clients can expect from live-in care and how it can benefit them.

Many people have asked me about live-in care: how to get a live-in care job, what it entails, what qualifications one needs, etc. The idea of writing a handbook giving a no-frills guide to the ins-and-outs of live-in care work niggled away at me for a while, and then just took over!

The world of live-in care is unfamiliar territory for most people who embark on it. Carers come from all walks of life, from different backgrounds, and with different levels of education. If we're honest, most of us get into caring initially simply to make a living, and what better way than to be of service to another. If you are open to new experiences, and like the idea of expanding your life, money will be just one of the things you gain from live-in care. By stepping onto the track of live-in care, I suddenly found myself confronted with challenges I didn't expect, but over the years, I have learnt how to meet them head on.

I hope this book offers the newcomer to caring an understanding of the nitty-gritty part of the job. Each care position is unique, as is each carer (and client), so there is no *one* way to care for someone. To provide the reader with a balanced view of live-in care, I have gleaned information from my own experiences, as well as from of other carers.

Perhaps you won't resonate with everything in this book, and you may find some of the information difficult to accept. However, I encourage you to use it simply as a guide if you want to enter the world of live-in care. In the words of someone far wiser than me – *'take whatever it is that strikes you and leave the rest.'*

A note on pronouns – I have used different pronouns to include everyone – she, he, and them. Sometimes it's him, and other times her, and then again it could be them.

CARERS COME FROM MANY CULTURES AND BACKGROUNDS

- 1 -

THE BASICS OF LIVE-IN CARE

'Nobody cares how much you know until they know how much you care.' - **Theodore Roosevelt**

Finding Work in Live-In Care

To find work in the care industry, all you need do is go online, type in *live-in care work in the UK*, and you will find dozens of options. Some care agencies have been in the business for decades and are dependable as a work source. However, we all form our opinions through our own experiences, and what I may endorse as a good company to work with, another carer may have a different opinion. Word of mouth has always proven to be the best way to find work in this industry. In time, your own experience will guide your preference – be it private care, or through an agency, or both.[1]

Before you go down that rabbit hole, there are other criteria necessary to get a caring job in the UK. There are distinct types of care work, and as a live-in carer you will be offered various options, such as:

- **Companion Care** – self-explanatory as the client is usually still mobile and independent but may need company and assistance with some daily tasks such as household chores, cooking, driving, or taking the dog for a walk. However, there are as many variants to this description as there are people needing care. It may also include some personal care such as helping a client in and out of a bath, or getting dressed, for example.

- **Palliative or Complex Care** – this usually involves someone with a life-threatening illness. It is more hands-on care as the client may need help with personal hygiene, medication administration, and moving and handling (using equipment). Some may need assistance at mealtimes too.

---

[1] *https://www.liveincarejobs.co.uk/*

This kind of care could include clients who are living with cancer, Parkinson's Disease, Multiple Systems Atrophy (MSA), Multiple sclerosis (MS) or people with mobility issues, as well as stroke survivors.

- **Dementia/Alzheimer's Care** – this can be a real challenge depending on the severity of the dementia. Care could simply be companionship, but often it requires assistance with personal hygiene (bathing and dressing, continence care), mobility, and emotional support. And enormous amounts of patience. It is recommended to do courses specifically directed at dementia care.

- **Respite Care** – usually temporary care for someone who has come out of hospital, or to give time off to a family member who is the primary carer.

- **End-of-Life Care** – an incredibly special time to care for someone, and usually involves working with the family, as well as medical staff.

To be employed in any of these roles, you will need training. To begin with, you will need *core skills* in the expected levels of literacy, numeracy, and communication.

For all these positions, a carer needs be physically robust in body and mind. Some of the work can also be physically challenging.

Qualifications – much has changed over the years, and as live-in care is becoming the new buzzword in social care, a live-in care worker must have the necessary qualifications. Many of the care providers and agencies that have sprung up like wild mushrooms after good rains offer *basic induction training*. This usually takes a week where one learns the basics of caring. It would be advantageous to complete the *Care Certificate (theory training)* which can be done online[2]. There are many theory courses offered online, but the practical courses, *Moving and Handling* and CPR will have to be done in person.

---

[2]*Care certificate course - caredemy.co.uk.*

There is the *practical* side and the *theoretical* side of basic care. Most courses cover:

- **Personal Care** – Helping clients to get in and out of bed. How to wash and dress/undress a person who can no longer do so independently. Dental care is also a vital part of personal hygiene. Personal hygiene can include hair and nail care too. Because of possible infection if not properly done, cutting a client's nails is not advised. A podiatrist/chiropodist, a family member, or friend should do this. However, filing and painting nails is acceptable.

- **Continence Management** – pad changes and the use of incontinence equipment such as different types of catheters. Practical training is needed to be able to use the equipment.

- **Moving And Handling** – If the client has mobility issues, you as the carer must know how to use equipment such as hoists, wheelchairs, transfer boards and turntables, splints, slide sheets, and handling belts. The practical aspects of training will have to be done in person.

- **Safe Administration of Medication** – Most clients will be on some form of medication which the carer may be required to administer. You will learn how to do so safely.

- **First Aid Awareness** – A basic knowledge of first aid and CPR is necessary.

- **Mental Capacity** – some clients are not able to make decisions for themselves, which means the carer must liaise with family members or an appointed trusted person regarding their care.

- **Safeguarding of Vulnerable Adults** – you will need to understand the rights and needs of vulnerable adults and the responsibility of a carer in this regard.

- **Dementia Care** – this aspect of care is now being given a lot more attention and is a module of its own (see chapter on Dementia care).

- **Fire Training** – what to do in case of a fire in a client's home.

- **Knowledge of English** - being able to speak, read and write English is necessary for most care jobs in the UK.

- **Record Keeping** - some admin duties are usually expected, such as keeping a daily care report, recording medication administration, and changes to the care plan. These reports are written in English.

All the above are covered in the basic care course. However, live-in care also requires attributes such as *Common Sense, Patience, Empathy, Respectfulness, and Adaptability*.

Every client has their own care plan which is tailored to suit their individual needs and the duties of the live-in carer will be defined according to those needs. However, general duties as a live-in care worker usually include:

- **Dietary Needs and Cooking** – Every client wants a "good" cook. The prospect of cooking for clients often fills carers with dread as it is not easy to cook for someone other than yourself or your family. Fear not! What you don't know about wholesome home-cooked meals, you will learn as you go. Your repertoire of recipes will grow. Get to love the kitchen because it is a room you will spend a lot of time in. It is a place of nurture and sustenance. Buy an apron, sharpen your knife, and infuse the kitchen with delicious aromas!

- **Cleaning and Laundry Chores** – most of the time, it's described as 'light housework.' There may be a cleaner who pops in for an hour or two every so often, but your job as carer is to ensure that all the spaces you work and live in are kept clean and tidy, for example, bedrooms (yours and the client's), bathrooms, kitchen, and living areas. Light housework can also include watering the garden/ house plants, walking the dog, etc. However, this can vary from household to household, and it depends on what's stated in your contract. It usually falls on the carer to do the laundry and ironing too.

- **Shopping and Errands for the Household** – these days online shopping is commonly used, making life easier for live-in carers. In some households, the cleaner, housekeeper, or family member may oversee replenishing the pantry or a household kitty may be provided.

- **Emotional Support and Companionship** – this can be easy or challenging depending on the client's state of mind. However, it is an integral part of your role as a carer. Sometimes, you are the only person with whom your client interacts, so establishing a solid and trusting connection is important for both of you. There is no doubt that the bond that can develop between a carer and her client may cause friction with family members (or even a housekeeper who has been working for the client for many years).

It is important to understand the dynamics of these relationships. This is shaky ground because one can get caught up in all sorts of family dramas which have absolutely nothing, zilch, nada to do with your job description. Suddenly, you find yourself getting deep into the scrap – offering solutions, pointing out bad behaviour, choosing sides. By that time, it's a slippery slope. Put on the brakes, step back and remind yourself - this is not for me to fix.

But how do you offer emotional support without getting emotionally involved? Acknowledge what is being said, and if you just can't resist giving your opinion, simply say 'May I make a suggestion?' Don't negate what your client says. Set your boundaries when she badmouths others in the house – (usually a spouse, cleaner or a second care worker). Suggest that she take it up with the person concerned because it has nothing to do with you. You should not be expected to act as a go-between.

- **Health Issues** – the live-in carer may have to monitor a client's health issues such as diabetes and blood pressure, pressure sores, leg ulcers, cuts and scrapes, bruising. Fortunately, there is always a district nurse to call for support. These days, one can consult with the doctor via the internet services, which most surgeries offer, to get some advice.

- **Driving** – The job you take may require that you drive the client to appointments, meetings, or social events. You'll need to have a driver's licence that's valid in the UK. If using the client's car, then ensure you are added to their insurance. If you use your own car to drive your client somewhere, make sure you are properly covered by your insurance to do so.

- 2-

A WORD ON THE MONEY

'A wise man should have money in his head but not in his heart.' - **Jonathan Swift**

Like most people, live-in carers work to earn a living. Care work is a calling for some, but for many it is simply a means to an end, which hopefully is approached with a sense of care and responsibility. Unfortunately, it is an industry that has a reputation for underpaying workers. The issue of what is a fair salary can be tricky territory to navigate, especially if you are working privately.

Working privately - this is where your self-worth is tested. If you want to be paid what you think you deserve, now is the time to speak up because nobody else will do it for you. However, if you are anything like me and many people I know, talking about money elicits all kinds of emotions, insecurities, and doubts. The thought of approaching someone to say 'this is my fee' was like walking the plank for me - heart in mouth, drum beating in my head. But take it from one who has seen over the edge of that plank – negotiating for yourself is a most liberating experience. I showed up for myself, and owned control of my finances. What I discovered was that there were no shark-infested waters, only the clear spring of relief and resolve. Dive right in, the water is fine!

Working with an introductory agency – any introductory agency worth its salt will negotiate a fair and reasonable rate with the client on your behalf. However, the contract is between you and the client, *not* between you and the agency. What is considered a fair rate? Most care rates are gauged by the level of care involved and the experience of the carer. Agencies usually quote for a *10-12-hour day* live-in care and the rate can vary greatly; anything from *£100 per day to £150 per day* or more. There is usually a higher rate caring for couples. Private carers set their own rates and conditions of care. It is best to check the current rates before setting your fee. It is important to note that even though you are working through an introductory agency, you are considered *self-employed* for tax purposes and as such you do not have the same rights as someone who is an employee. Make sure your rate of pay and annual increases are stipulated in your contract.

If you're fully employed with an agency, your pay rate will be set by the agency, and you'll usually be paid weekly or bi-weekly.

THE BRIDGE PLAYER

- 3 -

REALITIES OF LIVE-IN CARE

'Caring for others is the highest expression of humanity.' **- Harriet Beecher Stowe**

One of the most asked questions about live-in care is *'What's it like?'* There are as many answers as there are carers. It's a unique work environment – you are working in the intimate space of someone's home in which you, as carer, are expected to keep clean and tidy, prepare meals in someone else's kitchen, do their laundry and ironing, as well as act as companion, entertainer, and be a good, passive listener who offers no opinions. It is a massive adjustment for the client to have to relinquish control of their home to a total stranger. Naturally, you may meet lots of resistance. It could mean working with a person who may push your buttons, repeat themselves over and over, and be demanding, bossy, rude, weepy, or wonderful. Then again, you may be lucky enough to find yourself caring for someone with a fabulous sense of humour, who is kind, considerate, appreciative, and grateful to have you in their lives.

It really is the luck of the draw, but a lot depends on your attitude. You will be challenged many times and discover to your amazement just how resilient you are, be surprised at your level of patience, be humbled by your lack of understanding, feel the tingle of newfound knowledge, and recognize the patina of experience you have earned. It will highlight your strengths and expose your weaknesses. You will be expected to do things you never imagined you'd ever do. You will be confronted by your own limiting beliefs. You will come to understand what it means to be flexible, resourceful, and astute.

It is helpful to enter your assignment with no expectations, an open heart, and a positive attitude. Remember that holistic care – that of the mind, body and soul is the best care you could offer someone.

Here are a few challenges you will face:

- Occupying just one room in a stranger's house and living out of a suitcase or more, depending on how much you want to carry with you.

- Moving from one client to another.

- Having to cook meals to the taste of your client rather than your own.

- Living according to someone else's rhythm rather than your own.

- Being indoors for most of the day with limited free time.

- Dealing with the responsibility of administering prescribed medication.

- Assisting the client with personal hygiene care.

- Caring for someone with a different language and culture to your own.

- Being micro-managed by the client, family members, housekeeper or even the client's friends.

- Experiencing a rollercoaster of emotions.

These are all things you may have to deal with at one time or another as a live-in carer. We humans are resilient and adaptable, and so it won't take long for you to settle into some kind of routine for yourself. Give yourself time, be kind to yourself.

- 4 -

A STATE OF INDEPENDENCE

Respecting a client's lifestyle

'Life's most persistent and urgent question is – what are you doing for others?' **- Martin Luther King**

We come into people's lives as carers when they are frail, vulnerable, and often dependent on the help of someone else – someone like *you. But it was not always like that.* Before their health was compromised - be it memories stolen from them by dementia, or mobility lost or stricken by chronic illness, most clients would have lived vibrant, dynamic lives. Just look at the photos on the mantelpiece, or those gathering dust on the piano, or following you along the walls of the staircase. Notice the golf trophies, the Women's Institute awards, the souvenirs of travels to exotic destinations, and the library of photo albums marked by year – Alaska 1952, Lima 1956, Iceland 1968, Venezuela 1973, Everest 1999. There are pics of family members who they may no longer recognize - their grandson has become "a sweet young man" who visits occasionally, or their daughter who they now believe is their sister. It's important to remember that life wasn't always like this, and coping with the changes that age and illness have foisted on them is challenging enough, let alone having to come to terms with needing full-time care.

Your role as a live-in care worker is to:

- Enable people who need care and support to live in their own homes, maintain their daily routines and live as independently as possible, as well as offering them peace of mind by having 24/7 care on hand.

- Help with daily tasks such as at mealtimes, bathing, and dressing, personal care, moving and handling (using equipment if necessary) and administering medication.

- Assist with light housekeeping including laundry and ironing.

- In some cases, manage the running of the household.

Your aim as a live-in care worker is to improve the quality of life of the client and help to maintain as much independence and dignity as possible. It is not to take over their lives. People who have been diagnosed with neurological disorders such as Parkinson's Disease or Dementia, may well be capable of doing many things, albeit slowly. This can be quite frustrating to an able-bodied person, and the temptation to do it for them is what we need to resist. If we don't, then we are taking away their independence. It is sometimes difficult to discern the difference between someone needing help, or just being slow. There are certain activities that are harder than others, such as buttoning shirts (finicky small buttons are a nightmare). putting on trousers or bending down to tie shoelaces. Take your cue from your client, and if she is able to communicate, simply ask if she needs help with something.

The live-in carer's presence in someone's life is to help them maintain as much independence as possible, while at the same time being the support that they may need. It is a fine balance between the two.

KEEPING RECORDS IS PART OF LIVE-IN CARE DUTIES

- 5 -

PLANNING AND PREPARATION

Requirements for working in the UK.

'Leadership is not about being in charge. Leadership is about taking care of those in your charge.' - **Simon Sinek**

This chapter concentrates on information about working in the UK and comes from my experience as a live-in care worker in England. However, all the tenets of caring are applicable in most countries.

THE RIGHT TO WORK IN THE UK.

You need to have one of the following to work in the UK:

- British citizenship.

- Ancestral visa. If your grandparents were born in the UK, you qualify for an ancestral visa. This is a very costly exercise, and you need plenty of documentation, but it is worth the stress and expense.

- Sponsorship from an agency or company. There are all sorts of conditions linked to sponsorship.

- Valid work visa.

- EU passport holders also require a visa.

If you have one of the above then *voilà*, you can continue the process. You need to be legally allowed to live and work in the UK to do live-in care. Acquiring this status if you are not a British subject can be time consuming and arduous, requiring plenty of documentation. Visit the UK government website (https://www.gov.uk) for more information.

- **Police Clearance** - you will need this from your country of residence in order to get an **Enhanced Disclosure and**

Barring Certificate (DBS) to work in the UK. You are unlikely to get a job without a DBS. It allows an employer to check whether you have a criminal record. It would be best to get the police clearance certificate from your country of residence *before* leaving for the UK. Check with your local police station. Applications for an enhanced DBS certificate must be done by an employer, and if a care company employs you, they can assist you with the application. However, if you decide to work as a *self-employed live-in carer*, it is your responsibility to ensure you have this document. You can get help through NACAS (The National Association for Carers and Support Workers). (See Useful Links and References).

- **Carer insurance/public liability** - You will need some form of insurance if you are working privately or through an introductory agency. It's as much about protecting yourself against nasty claims as it is about making claims if something happens to you. There are several insurance companies who have specific insurance for carers, and you can access them online. Just type in 'insurance for live in carers' and they'll pop up. Fish Insurance and Surewise are two I have used in the past. Expect to pay around £100 a year.

- **UK bank account** - You will need to open a bank account in the UK and register with HMRC for a Unique Tax Reference number (UTR) and apply for a National Insurance number (NI). You have to register for this through the government website. Some agencies assist with this, but if you are going private, then check the UK government and HMRC websites online.

- **UK address as domicile** – You need to have an address in the UK in order to do all of the above. This is where friends and family who live in the UK come in handy, as you could stay with them and request that all correspondence be sent to their address. You will need their permission to do so.

- **Letter of Employment or contract** – It does make life easier

If you are coming to the UK on an ancestral visa or going the sponsorship route, to organise work before you leave your country of residence.

Types of care agencies

Although there are thousands of home care agencies in the UK, there are only two types – full employment agency and introductory agency.

Full Employment Care Agency - you are fully employed with the company on a *contractual basis* which can be a zero-hour contract (no work, no pay), or on a pay as you earn basis (PAYE).

The advantages of working for a full employment care agency are:

- The agency sources the clients for you.

- The agency pays you directly.

- The agency is responsible for submitting your tax return on your behalf.

- You get holiday pay when you take leave, and you're entitled to sick pay.

- The agency must contribute towards a pension for you.

- The agency organises replacement carers when you go away.

- The agency is obliged to sort out any problems that may arise regarding a care position.

The disadvantages of working for a full employment agency are:

- You are accountable to not only your client, but also to the agency.

- You must follow their rules pertaining to record keeping.

- The agency sets the pay rate.

Introductory Care Agency - the agency acts as an *intermediary* between the client and carer, and you are contracted to the client as *self-employed*. There are varying levels of support or assistance for the carer in terms of resolving conflict that might arise between client and carer - change of care, working hours, etc., depending on the policy of the agency,

The advantages of working through an introductory agency are:

- You can choose your working times.

- The agency sources clients for you and creates a contract which you both sign.

- The agency is responsible for finding a replacement carer when you go on a break.

- Some agencies provide support in resolving conflict.

The disadvantages of working through an introductory agency are:

- You are responsible for submitting your tax returns and paying National Insurance yourself.

- As you are considered self-employed, you are responsible for invoicing your client.

- There is no holiday pay, sick pay, or pension - you have to budget for that yourself.

Private care work – this is similar to the above except you have to do *everything yourself* – find the work and negotiate with the client or the person entrusted with their care. If you decide to work this way, make sure you have your signed contract in place *before* work begins. Creating a contract is extremely important for your protection as a private live-in carer. Having a contract in place is a form of self-respect as it shows you are serious about what you do and know your worth. It is an agreement between you and the client on what you can do, are willing to do, and how much you expect to be paid for your services. When you sign on the dotted line you are making a commitment to uphold your end of the contract.

The advantages of working privately are:

- You are your own boss, so you choose when to work, where to work and with whom.

- You earn more than if you were working for an agency because you can negotiate a higher rate of pay. The client does not have any agency fees to pay.

The disadvantages of working as a private carer in the live-in care sector are:

- Because you are self-employed, you are not protected by employment law which means you do not automatically have the same rights as other workers. You forfeit the right to the National Minimum Wage, statutory sick pay and contesting unfair dismissal.

- You must source your own clients and negotiate directly with them.

- You do not get holiday pay, pension, or sick pay.

- You must submit your own tax returns and pay National Insurance.

Many carers start out working with agencies, and after gaining some experience and forming a network of support, they move into the private care sector.

The contract – You can create your own contract if you are not using agencies. The salient points of a contract are:

- Fees and expenses – state your rate and how you would like payment to be made – weekly, bi-monthly, or monthly. Remember to include an annual pay increase in your contract.

- Place of work

- Working hours and time off

- Services and expectations

- Duration and termination

- A probationary period

- Open and honest communication

- Personal conduct – be respectful, courteous, non-discriminatory.

- Carer to have relevant qualifications and enhanced DBS.

- Adhere to any health and safety regulations.

- Confidentiality

Work through sponsorship

There has been a lot of bad press lately about this means of finding work as a carer in the UK. After the fallout of Brexit, staff shortages became an ugly reality in the care industry. In an attempt to rectify this, the government created a *Health and Care worker visa* with a sponsorship scheme, whereby foreign workers could apply to work in the UK.

However, it is primarily to fill posts within the NHS and only approved employers can offer sponsorship. This seems to be a route fraught with potholes, pitfalls, and a lot of disappointment. One has to jump through many hoops to get here.

For those wishing to negotiate this route, this is what you will need:

- A Health and Care worker visa and a 'certificate of sponsorship' from a government approved employer in the UK.

- A proven knowledge of English – either by passing a Secure English Language Test (SELT) or having a degree taken in English and equivalent to any BA, MA or PHD degree received in the UK.

- A qualification in the care industry – either as a doctor, nurse, health professional or adult social care professional.

The cost of a 3-year visa application can be more than £300 and a longer visa will be more expensive. Fee prices change, so get the latest from the UK government website.

You will need a *stipulated minimum amount of funds in your bank account* to be able to support yourself for a month in the UK. You will need a *biometric resident permit* which has to be done through an approved visa application centre. You will have to apply through the UK government website and approval usually takes about three weeks. [1]

International Driving Licence – if you do not come from an EU country, you will need this permit to drive in the UK.

---

[1] *https://www.gov.uk/health-care-worker-visa/apply-from-outside-the-uk*

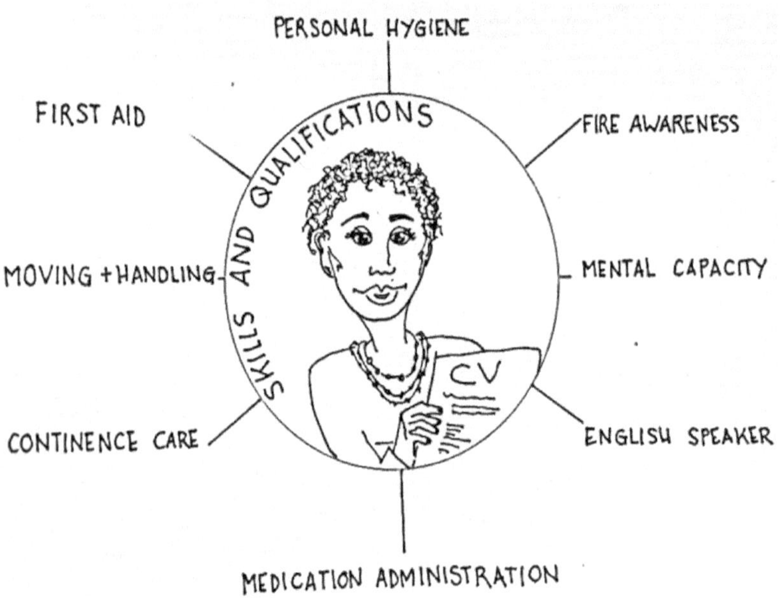

THE SKILLS AND QUALIFICATIONS YOU WILL NEED TO DO LIVE-IN CARE

- 6 -

THE INTERVIEW

'As you grow older, you will discover that you have two hands – one for helping yourself, and the other for helping others.' **- Maya Angelou**

These days interviews for care work are sometimes done in person, but more often online. A face-to-face interview can be very intimidating but you can make it less so by being prepared in every way - mind (formulate your answers ahead of time), body (look your best) and soul (be true to yourself). If it's an online interview, best to get out of the pj's, tidy up and brush your hair! As a wise person once said: 'Dress like you would like to be addressed!'

There will be some standard questions such as *'Why do you want to be a carer?'* For many people, money is the great motivator, yet somehow saying that aloud in an interview may sound more callous than caring. Think about this question in depth beforehand and answer the question for yourself, *'Why do I want to be a carer? What are my aims and objectives?'* If you answer these questions honestly, then you will discover a lot about yourself that may well have been hidden in the recesses of self-doubt and denial.

However, even with the best of intentions, the reality of life does not always pan out the way we imagined, and you will find yourself reassessing your responses when doing the job.

The next question may be *'Why do you think you would make a good carer?'* A trickier question to answer for some perhaps. A few predictable responses are *'Because I like old people.' 'Because I want to be of service.' Then come the* clichéd *'I'm kind, caring, gentle, considerate, patient.'* Great attributes, *but* these are the very parts of you that will be tested repeatedly in caring. When your client has told you the same story in exactly the same words for the umpteenth time, or accused you of trying to poison her while administering medication, or suspects you of stealing from her, then *kind, gentle, considerate and patient* morph into *teeth gnashing, nose itching, I-just-want-to-scream moments*. When you've been summarily dismissed with a flick of the wrist and told to 'close the door softly behind you,' then *patient and understanding* are replaced by *silent rage and indignation*. When the meal you have prepared is pushed aside with the comment: '*I can't eat that, it tastes awful,*' it may take every ounce of resistance not to dump the plate right on his lap.

It is difficult to think kind thoughts when clients are being impossibly demanding, but uttering unkind thoughts would be inexcusable.

Often, we can feel angry at ourselves and guilty for feeling the way we do, but it is important to remind ourselves that the reason for the client's 'challenging' behaviour, is because of their illness, condition, or disease. It is not personal.

Some people do have infinite patience, are always gentle, kind, and considerate. They are called earth angels. But we humans are like diamonds – multi-faceted and exquisite while catching the light, but also dark and fathomless when not. Remember that whatever is happening will eventually pass...

Another question might be '*Have you ever cared for someone?*' Most of us have in some way, be it looking after children, visiting grannies, shopping for aunties and uncles, checking on an older neighbour or parent. You may have experienced some element of caring, but live-in care takes it to another level.

Take some time to consider these questions and answer them honestly and with integrity to yourself *before* the interview. That way you will have a better understanding of what you expect of yourself as a carer. When considering what makes a good carer, the **6Cs** come into play:

COMPASSION

CARE

COMPETENCE

COURAGE

COMMUNICATION

COMMITMENT

and then add in their cousin,

KINDNESS

- 7 -

GETTING SET UP IN THE UK

'From caring comes courage.' **- Lao Tzu**

So now, you have gone through the interview and been offered a job. Well done! Yet you find yourself waking up in the middle of the night in a cold sweat, heart pumping, full of doubt. Suddenly you realise that not only are you going to care for someone as a professional carer, but you will be doing so in another country. That means a whole new way of moving in the world; negotiating public transport, getting connected to a mobile phone network, opening a bank account, dealing with tax. Here are some of the service providers that you can use in the UK.

Mobile Networks

- EE
- O2
- THREE
- Vodafone, and more.
- Public Transport
- National Express Bus Service
- British Rail
- Banks
- Lloyds Bank
- HSBC
- Barclays
- NatWest, and many more.

Medical Care for You

As a carer, you will have different assignments in various parts of the country. This makes it challenging when having to seek medical care as the system in the UK is to register with the surgery where you live. You will have to register with a surgery near you as *a temporary* patient (less than 3 months) if you want to have access to medical care while working. The way to do this is to visit the local surgery (the one your client uses is a good start) and register with them. These days, registration is normally done online. Find out the necessary information from the local surgery.

Storage

Another aspect of live-in care that will rear its ugly head after some time is where, oh where, to store the excess baggage you have. And you will have it: the heavy winter boots and coats that you don't want to be carrying around with you in the summer months, for example. Or the extra full suitcase you don't need while working. Or all the books you've bought and just can't let go of. All far too much to be dragging upstairs at a train station, that's for sure!

There are storage facilities all over Britain and prices vary, depending on the size of the storage unit and the area. Another alternative is to make use of bag collection and delivery services such as Send My Bag and LOVESPACE which offer not only storage facilities but also collection and delivery. You can find more info on the internet about these services. (see Useful Links and References).

Accommodation during breaks

There will be times when you need a break from caring, or there'll be some time in between assignments when you need somewhere to stay. Some carers are fortunate to have family they can go to and spend time with, but many of us don't. Where to go? This would the time to explore your new world, so if you're on a budget, B+Bs are a viable choice, as are backpacker hostels which are great for meeting new people. There are also fellow carers who live in the UK and rent out rooms in their homes at fair rates. They advertise through social media (see Useful Links and References).

OUR CLIENTS HAVE HAD A LIFETIME OF
EXPERIENCES OF WHICH WE KNOW NOTHING

- 8 -

WHAT CARE WORKERS SAY ABOUT LIVE-IN CARE

'No one is useless in this world who lightens the burden of it to anyone else.' **- Charles Dickens**

The human experience is such that we have many things in common, but how we experience life depends on our characters and our environment. We are all individuals and we each tackle life with the tools we have been given. So, what have the people who have been working in live-in care learnt from their experiences? Here are some of their comments:

Yonna says working as a live-in carer has given her the gift of staying in the moment, and of humility. 'Just when I'm at the end of my tether, patience worn thin, and I am swirling in a vortex of stinking thinking, my client takes my hand and says, 'thank you for taking care of me.' I see this as a gentle reminder to be mindfully present, and that ego has no place in this line of service. I felt that the biggest challenge for me was to find my own rhythm and routine, while having to live according to my client's. It is crucial for one's state of mind. The other important lesson I have had to learn is *not to take things personally*. Caring can become a battle of wills, and I have learnt to take the path of least resistance in dealing with complex human beings.'

Gerda is a woman who has stood up to fate with the ferociousness of a true warrior. Her advice to the new carer is to 'leave your beliefs and opinions at the front door! Be secure in the knowledge of what you can offer, and don't be afraid to ask for advice or support from the caring community. Be humble enough to listen to NHS staff but advocate for your client in a respectful manner.

'Be cautious about disclosing too much information about yourself to the client and their circle of influence. The client pays for your professional services, *not* for the fodder of gossip sessions with their family and friends. Be friendly and caring but maintain a professional distance – it makes for a more harmonious arrangement. Remember, you are there to provide your client with the opportunity to live as independently as possible, so don't try to do everything and make yourself indispensable. You are not.'

When asked what she learnt from live-in care, **Sarah** said: 'I learnt about myself and how compassionate I am, and of my need to help people. It humbled me in a good way. I also made life-long friendships with incredible people. I learnt routine, and to care unconditionally, to the best of my ability, for those who needed me. I met people from all walks of life. It taught me to appreciate and give the best to my own family.'

For **Ruth**, the keyword is *detachment*. 'A carer needs to maintain a certain degree of detachment and recognise that you can only do what you can do. You can't wave a magic wand. You must have balance, and not give your whole being over, otherwise you come out of the experience depleted. Your client is not your family, so be mindful of not getting emotionally entangled in their affairs. It is important to remember that clients are adults, and they have the right to make their own decisions and choices, if they still have mental capacity to do so. It is irrelevant whether you think it is right or wrong. As a carer, you are trying to give them the freedom to live the best life they can, and the carer's job is to be in the background, to make it as safe as possible for them to do that.'

Lynne, who has been caring for several years, advises the newcomer to live-in care on how to combat loneliness. 'Make sure your client has good Wi-Fi – not negotiable! Use technology to chat to family and friends. Contact fellow carers and arrange regular meetups.'

She also warns against being bullied. 'Bullying by clients or their family, or an agency, is something to be aware of.

If you are unhappy in your job because the client is rude and abusive, leave. Find work where you feel valued, not just in words but in salary too.'

Adaptability is one attribute that **Skye** found in caring. 'You must adapt to different households and cultures. Another vital aspect of live-in care is finding time for yourself, as well as maintaining your mental health. We are just passing feathers in the wind, so to conquer isolation, it is important to create a relationship with yourself because you are the one constant.'

For **Louise,** it is about *connection and knowledge*. 'Do training courses to better equip yourself for the job. Learn as much as you can about your client's health issues - what is required, and what to avoid.' She believes that connecting with the broader caring community is important. 'Exchanging phone numbers with other carers and people who understand the work you do, is a good means of support. Take care of yourself too – wake up early, have 'me' time, get outdoors and exercise daily, even if it's just a short walk. Self-love is important for you to give of yourself in helping others.'

Working as a live-in carer has given **Rachel** a *sense of freedom of choice* as to when she works, and for how long. 'Although I love and enjoy caring, taking breaks from the job is necessary, especially if one is working with a client who has a debilitating condition like dementia, or Parkinsons, or MS. Coming from another country to work in the UK. I have also experienced financial freedom, and can do more with my money, travel, and enjoy life more, which I wasn't able to do as easily back home.'

Bev, who has been caring for 10 years, has learnt to appreciate her own health, to be grateful for it, and to look after herself. 'I have also learnt that I'm a lot more capable, empathetic, and organised than I thought I was. It's not so scary. I have discovered that you can do pretty much anything if you have disposable gloves on! It's hard to see older people suffer and struggle, as many do, to do things that we take for granted. I tend to think of my own mom when I'm caring. and think how I would like her to be treated – gently, respectfully and with patience.'

'Being a carer has also given me the freedom to travel more often. I've worked all over the UK and Channel Islands. Caring has enabled me to see places I probably would never have got to if I weren't caring.'

Bev, like so many other carers, has learned that boundaries are important in this line of work. 'There will always be the client who will push you to the limit. That is when you need to stand up for yourself.'

WATCH WHAT YOU SAY
HAVE A CONTRACT
TAKE CARE OF YOURSELF
DON'T TAKE THINGS PERSONALLY
KEEP RECORDS
ACCEPTANCE
BREATHE!
STICK WITH THE PROGRAM
PERSONAL CARE
ATTITUDE
10 LESSONS OF CARE

- 9 -

TEN LESSONS FOR LIVE-IN CARE

'Love and compassion are necessities not luxuries. Without them, humanity cannot survive.' **- The Dalai Lama**

In this job you are collaborating with a real live human being in their own home. The dynamics can get interesting for both the carer and the client. You, as the carer, are entering someone else's home, which is decorated and designed to suit her needs, not yours. Her waking hours may not be the same as yours, and her eating habits and mealtimes may be way out of sync with your own. The urge to change things can become quite overwhelming, and you will try to rationalise and justify the need to rearrange things. You may find yourself working in a home in which the family has lived for generations, where there are volumes of books three rows deep on every shelf, and a coat of dust that adds a layer on top! There may be precious ornaments on every ledge, table, and mantelpiece. Faded family photos in grubby frames placed higgledy-piggledy on a piano that belonged to great-great grandmamma. There may be tins of food in the pantry bearing labels that date back to before you were born, and sheets in the linen cupboard that have been nibbled by moths for years. You may also care for someone who has a different culture to yours, and the way things are done might not make any sense to you.

You will suddenly discover the obsessive-compulsive side of your nature and find it difficult to resist the urge to rearrange the furniture, reorganise the crockery, repack the bookshelves, and redo the linen cupboard 'because it would be better.' And you may well be right, but it may not seem necessary to the client.

Lesson one - Acceptance

This is not your house. Leave well alone! One of the hardest parts of live-in care is to accept the ways of the client. You will be faced with weird and not so wonderful patterns of living. Each household is different, and as a carer you must respect that.

Lesson two – Take good care of yourself

In a companion care assignment, there is often time in the day when the client is doing something that does not involve you, but if summoned, you need to heed the call. So, when all your immediate chores are done, and your client is busy, how do you pass the time while waiting for the call to duty? You could grab a book and read, but it *could also* be an opportunity to draft your *own* book or discover your hidden talents. Bring out the crochet hooks and knitting needles, the drawing kit, the embroidery hoops. Welcome to the world of *creativity!* And when the bell rings, you can just put it all down and get back to work. Easy-peasy! It's a great idea to find a creative outlet, which allows you to roam in the realm of imagination rather than flounder in a whirlpool of worry and angst. It stops you from falling into the pit of isolation and loneliness, regret, and frustration – common in live-in care. Creative space is a magical place to be because you are doing something for *yourself*.

Also, ensure you are getting *enough exercise and nourishment.* The nature of the job is to take care of someone else, and often it can be at the expense of your own health. Carers who do not manage their self-care well can suffer from what is known as *compassion fatigue. Be mindful not to neglect yourself.*

For those of you who like to be part of a group or organisation, there are carer WhatsApp groups, and Facebook groups through which you can interact with other live-in carers. In the UK, there are organisations such as: **NACAS** *(National*

Association of Care and Support Workers)[1] which celebrates and supports the social care workforce. It also hosts a Voluntary Care Professional Register (VCPR)[2] for care professionals in England, and any self-employed carers who want to be on the register. For more information, check out their websites (see Useful Links and References).

The Care Workers Union (CWU) is a newly formed trade union specifically focused on 'advancing care workers' rights and working conditions.' It is a paid membership, and you can learn more about this union by visiting its website[3]

Here is a *Self-Care* checklist that you can practice every day:

- Begin your day with meditation or prayer.

- Morning exercise.

- Eat fruit and veggies.

- Keep hydrated – water is the elixir of life.

- Practice gratitude.

- Read for at least an hour a day from a book, not your phone.

- Keep your space neat and tidy.

- Do something creative.

- Spend time in nature.

- Spend time in good nurturing company.

Lesson three– Sticking with the programme

Like it or not, the nature of live-in care is such that there is a certain amount of 'light housekeeping' included in contracts. It would be good to clarify just what that entails before taking the job. Light housekeeping is generally accepted as keeping

---

[1] *https://www.nacas.org.uk/*

[2] *https://www.vcpr.co.uk/*

[3] *https://careworkersunion.org/the-care-workers-union/*

your workspaces clean and tidy - the kitchen, living area, the bedrooms, and bathrooms, as well as doing the laundry.

Then again, the client often expects you to do chores such as polish the silver, weed the garden, sweep the courtyard, mend clothing, run 'little' errands, or declutter the attic. Check your contract and put down your boundaries. You may well be one of those carers who, to stave off boredom, does not mind tackling duties that are considered outside the remit of care work. How very noble of you! *However*, if it is not in the contract, you are not obliged to do such tasks. If you do, you risk setting a precedent, and the client may expect the next carer to do the same. Having said that, it could well be a way to connect with your client if he is involved in the task as well, and if he is willing. Don't force the issue. Whatever you *choose* to do, do it with an open heart. Enjoy the process.

Lesson four – Count to ten

When it all gets too much, remember to *Stop. Breathe, Assess,* count to ten and remind yourself that *'this too shall pass'.'*

Lesson five – It's not about you, don't take things personally

There will be instances in your caring life when things are said and done that stab right through you – a glib comment about you being the hired help, or a remark about the clothes you are wearing, or criticism about the way you pronounce certain words. It could be that you walk too heavily on the wooden floor or are careless when washing the dishes. Depending what kind of day you're having (a tetchy client refusing to get dressed for an appointment, for example), these kinds of interactions can seem too much. The best advice is to count to ten, breathe deeply, and remember it really isn't about you. The client might also be having a down day. *Do not take it personally.* This is one of the hardest lessons to learn.

Some of us can't shut up when something irks us, and why should we if someone is treating us badly? If you feel put upon, exploited, or disrespected in your job, it is up to you to speak out. You and you alone must address the issue. Stand up for yourself. This is part of your self-care. The flip side to this lesson, of course is to watch your words – say what you have to say in a neutral tone and with kindness in your heart. Set your boundaries of what you will and will not accept. Sometimes this is easier said than done, but if you have the right intention, it works. And if you can't find the right words, then as my gran used to say: 'Save your breath to cool your porridge!'

One carer relates how, while working with a second carer, she was trying to get the client dressed and all the second carer was doing was chatting away to the client. She became irritated and said something brusquely about getting a move on. The second carer didn't react but responded in a firm yet gentle voice: 'That wasn't a very nice way to speak to *someone*.' It was the perfect response because she did not *personalise* her criticism, but simply made a statement which pulled the perpetrator up short and elicited a humble apology.

Lesson six– Listen carefully

As carers we need to be *mindful* of how we respond or react to what our client says and does. Many of us do not listen properly – with our full attention. We think we know what people want to say without letting them finish, especially if they are slow to explain, which can be the case with older people suffering from memory loss or speech problems. As a result, our responses to what is said or done may be inappropriate. Become aware of listening fully before responding.

Lesson seven – Be prepared for personal care

If you are anything like most of us, you would be balking at this subject right now. Personal care can include incontinence care, which means dealing with soiled undergarments and incontinence pads. There is nothing pleasant about it, yet it is often a necessary part of live-in care jobs. Surprisingly, one does get used to it!

Can you imagine how demeaning and undignified it must feel for the person in need of such care? Ask yourself this question: *How would I feel being the one on the receiving end?* How you manage yourself as a carer can help your client feel more at ease and comfortable with what must be done to maintain their dignity. Think about how you would like to be treated if it were you on that bed. The best way of getting it over with as quickly as possible is to *be prepared* so that what you must do is done without fuss. Have everything you need within easy reach. Although most care training courses do cover incontinence care, it will benefit you (and your client) to check out some of the informative YouTube videos about incontinence care. Then prep your workspace, put on your gloves and apron, fill a bowl with warm water, fold that flannel in four, and get on with it!

If possible, it is important that the client does their own personal hygiene, but if you suspect they are not doing it very well, you may have to have a conversation with them about it. Urinary tract infections (UTIs) can happen because of bad hygiene, and that can lead to all sorts of other problems best avoided. Have the conversation in a respectful, caring manner. If you feel you're not up to it, or the client refuses talk about it, then ask a family member or district nurse/doctor to do so.

Lesson eight – Co-operation makes it happen (two carer positions)

You may find yourself on an assignment that requires two carers, which usually means caring for someone who has mobility issues and may also be bed bound. It often involves using moving and handling equipment, some of which requires two carers to manage. Some carers choose to work in a two-carer position because of the company it offers. Often carers form solid friendships in two-carer positions. It can even be fun if both carers respect each other and are willing to share the responsibilities and duties of care for their client.

Conflict can become an issue when working in a two-carer position - *there's my way, her way, and the client's way*. It is humbling for a carer to learn that her way is not the only or best way to do something. She may be teamed up with another carer who thinks the same about her own method of care. That spells trouble with a capital T. A battle of wills ensues, creating a nasty vibe while they 'arm-wrestle' to see who gets her way. Obviously, you should speak out if what the other carer is doing is dangerous or hurtful to the client, but otherwise, step back, watch, and you may learn something new. However, if you find yourself working with a co-worker who is mean to the client, bullies you, and creates unpleasantness by being uncooperative and demanding, speak out!

The Golden Rule: Never argue in front of the client. It is important to remember that your client is your priority, and to accept that every carer has her own way of doing things. Acceptance is the key unless what the carer is doing is abusive or disrespectful to the client. Then you have a duty of care to address the situation. The ideal would be to reach some sort of compromise.

It can be extremely fulfilling to have a co-worker with whom you resonate, and it is amazing how things flow as each one knows how the other works and what is expected of them. Everything works in synchronicity. It's magic for the carers and gold for the client.

An advantage to two-carer work is that there is someone else to share the responsibility of care, and in some cases, provides much needed company. If you work well together, and get on as individuals, the life of a two-carer position can be quite appealing.

Lesson nine – Working with couples, dealing with families

Carers are often required to manage various aspects of the home apart from care management. If a boiler (geyser) goes on the blink for example, the carer may be the one to organise its repair. If the light bulb blows, it will usually be the carer who will have to change it. When the central heating plays up in the middle of winter, the carer will normally be the one who has to phone for help.

Any problems that arise in the home where the person being cared for is unable to solve them, are usually left up to the carer to resolve. However, the family may also take on that responsibility. Each care position is different. A family member usually organises the economic management of a household, giving the carer a weekly budget to work with, or sometimes the use of a debit card to buy groceries and other household goods. The important thing to remember is to keep a record of *all* expenses.

Working with family members does have its challenges. Often relatives are not involved in any meaningful way on a daily basis with their relative's care, so they have no idea what life is really like in the home. Some just do not care – the weight of responsibility having been shifted onto the carer. This can be very frustrating and affect the level of care offered their loved ones by their refusing to do, or buy, what is needed to make life easier for the client. If you are working through an agency, then get them to speak to the family members or trusted person. If you're self-employed and are concerned that your client is being neglected because of the family's reluctance to provide for their needs, then it becomes a safeguarding issue and you should report your concerns to a relevant authority – the client's doctor, a social worker, or the police.

Most families do keep in touch with their loved one regularly, visiting often, asking questions, and listening to the carer. They understand that they are an integral part of the care team. They show appreciation and respect for the carer.

Carer, not marriage counsellor

One aspect of couple caring that you should be aware of is not to involve yourself in the dynamics of the couple. This can be a tricky business, especially if it is a dysfunctional relationship. You will be witness to behaviour that has been formed over years, often decades. In the case of one in the couple being the client in need of help, the attitude of the spouse can play a vital role in the wellbeing of the client. How that person reacts to and communicates with the client will have an effect.

As a carer, you must remember that whatever disability your client has, be it a progressive condition like Parkinson's disease or dementia which changes them, this impacts heavily on a relationship and the way the couple communicates. Often the spouse cannot cope with the changes to a loved one, and another side of their character emerges. They may get embarrassed and respond angrily or impatiently. For them it is like living with someone who looks like their spouse but seems to be a different person. It is important to acknowledge the effect that a client's deteriorating condition has on a spouse and family. Some do not know enough about whatever their family member is suffering from to understand its progress and deal with it. Very few get any kind of emotional support in dealing with this massive change in their life, as well as in their loved one's life.

As a carer in this situation, knowledge and compassion are essential - learn as much as possible about the condition your client has so that you can talk about it, reassure people, and prepare them, and yourself.

Lesson 10 – Beware of ableism

ABLEISM is the intentional or unintentional discrimination or oppression of individuals with disabilities.

We live in an ableist society in which we often don't even realise that we discriminate against those who live with a disability - be it mental, physical, or psychological - as well as those who live with a chronic illness.

 Some behaviours of ableism are:

- Shouting or speaking loudly to someone when it is not necessary.

- Talking for someone when they can speak for themselves.

- Talking about someone as if they are not in the room.

- Using body language in a negative way towards someone – making gestures behind their back, rolling one's eyes.

- Making exasperated sounds such as sighing loudly or huffing.

These are some of the things we need to watch out for in our behaviour when caring. The partner of a client thought that because he had power of attorney over his wife's affairs, he also had the right to speak for her, even though she still had mental capacity to respond herself. In that way, he excluded her from the discussion of her care, negated her opinion and made her feel, as she said, 'invisible.' This is also a form of control (especially for someone who may be feeling out of control of a situation he can do little to change). It causes unnecessary friction and conflict, and as the carer, you can find yourself in the middle of it all. This is known as gaslighting and is a form of ableism.

It is important when caring for someone who is disabled to be mindful of how we speak to them. There is no need to speak, louder, or in a 'baby' voice to people who may have dementia, or PD, or MS, or who have had a stroke, and therefore move more slowly and are slower to react. Always speak to them as the adult they are – clearly and to the point. And wait for a response.

It is not easy to hide the frustration and impatience one might feel towards a client when one is having a *bad* day, but behaviour such as negating what a client says, or huffing loudly when he wants to do something that seems unnecessary, or slamming a door in anger, is unacceptable.

There will be times when you are challenged in this way. Remember the rule: *Stop. Breathe. Assess.*

To sum up: Always maintain *your* self-respect by acting in a mindful, considerate, and compassionate manner when caring for a client.

If you do lose your cool and say (or do) something inappropriate, make sure that you apologise to your client as soon as possible.

- 10 -

INTERFERING vs CARING
– it's all about perception.

'Only a life lived for others is a life worthwhile.' - **Albert Einstein**

Anyone who has cared for someone - be it a family member or a paying client, will no doubt have 'crossed a line' without intending to, and been accused of interfering in their affairs, their life, their home. It is all about perception. Often older people in need of assistance resist it out of pride or denial. So, any help offered is viewed as an interference when they may clearly need a hand. There is a fine balance between caring and interference.

As carers we are often faced with this dilemma. One of the traps we can easily fall into is to try to make life easier for the client by doing things that they still may want to or are able to do themselves, albeit slowly. That may well be seen as interfering instead of caring. A way to stop this confusion is to be clear in your communication about your intention. Ask yourself, 'is this interfering or is it caring?'

Always ask your client if they want help before trying to help them. Never impose your opinions or your actions on your client – instead, ask if you can 'make a suggestion,' thereby giving them the option of accepting your help or not.

Sometimes the need to intervene is necessary, for example when the client becomes confused by a phone call that is clearly a scam call. It would be remiss of you not to try to stop the call. However, how you do that will be the difference between interfering and caring. Depending on the lucidity of your client, it may take a while to explain your actions so that they are appreciated instead of resented. Another tricky situation is when the client gives incorrect information to someone, be it relating an incident to a friend, or describing symptoms to a doctor, or explaining something to a relative. Is it right to correct them? Is it necessary? And how to do so?

It really depends on what the information is about. If it is idle chit-chat, ask yourself, does it really matter? But if it is essential information about the client's medication or condition that is being incorrectly remembered and therefore wrongly relayed, then it is necessary to intervene. It is important to approach the situation with gentleness and tact. It is also necessary to write about it in the daily care report.

You are bound to be confronted with this dilemma at some time in your caring life. And sometimes, it may well be that you are interfering. *Stop. Breathe. Assess.*

- 11 -
ARRIVALS AND DEPARTURES
The handover

'Respect goes a long way. If you've got no respect, you've got no gravity.' - **Hilton Ruiters**

The nature of live-in care work is such that you will be assigned to a client for a certain time. Usually, you have a say in how long you would like the assignment to be.

It could range from just a week to replace a carer, or it could be months at a time. Some carers like to work to a schedule of two weeks on-two weeks off, while others prefer to move from one client to the next after a few weeks. There are carers who have managed to build a relationship with their client and stay on for years, having breaks when needed. And are breaks needed! Find your balance of work and play. A decent work schedule for me is eight weeks on and two weeks off. By then I have managed to establish a rapport with my client so that when I return there is a sense of familiarity. It also depends on the intensity of the work that will determine your staying power.

If you are working through an agency, you may not have the same freedom of choice you have when you work privately. You also may not always get to choose where you work, whereas as a private carer you can choose your location and look for work in that area.

When you are given an assignment, it is important to liaise with the outgoing carer to synchronise arrival and departure times. There is usually a handover period in which the outgoing carer shows the incoming carer the ropes and explains the care plan. Organising these changeover times can be challenging, especially if carers are going from one job immediately to another. If there is some hitch or delay in departure, arrival at the next posting will be affected. This is when communication is imperative as the outgoing carer may well be heading to another assignment. Getting to an assignment on time is important.

It is also necessary to take time to show the incoming carer how things are done before leaving an assignment. Out of respect for the client and the replacement carer, do not rush this process. One way to manage the handover effectively is to make a handover list – room by room. Sometimes incoming carers can get caught up in waffling on about the traffic, or the previous assignment, or waste time unpacking their car. Try to stick to the handover information to make the transition as brief as possible. Most times, the outgoing carer prefers not to dillydally and to get going as soon as possible.

Show good manners and respect by ensuring that you leave your bedroom neat and tidy, with clean linen on the bed for the incoming carer. Sort out the fridge (no undated leftovers), clean the oven, and ensure that all records are up to date, as well as any finances, such as the household kitty.

It is important to establish whether you are the principal carer in a private care position. If so, it may be your responsibility to find a relief carer to cover your breaks. What sometimes happens is that the relief carer may want to extend her time and may try to manipulate the work roster to suit her own ends, which creates a tricky situation. It puts the client in an awkward position trying to accommodate both carers. It also doesn't bode well for good relations between the principal carer and the replacement carer, because it puts the principal carer in the position of having to insist that they stick to the agreed work roster.

To summarise:

- Co-operation makes it happen.

- Make a handover list.

- Leave the carer's bedroom neat and tidy with clean linen.

- Empty the fridge of old food and clean the stove/oven.

- Make sure all records are updated.

- Be punctual, and if you're running late, communicate this to the other carer.

AUGUSTE DETER

- 12 -
BEFORE I FORGET...
DEMENTIA CARE

'Caring is the bridge that connects us to one another.'
- Tich Nhat Hanh

In times gone by, when someone (usually an older person) displayed strange behaviour, such as claiming to see things that were clearly not there, or wandering around restlessly, or saying things that did not make sense at all, we called them *batty, senile, doolally, away with the fairies*, or words to that effect. Today this is considered inappropriate language. *People living with dementia* is the acceptable terminology. Dementia has been known to the medical world since the 18th century, but the first person to be diagnosed with a form of dementia, Auguste Deter was in the early 20th century (1901) by Dr Alois Alzheimer.

Dementia is not a disease; it is a condition that can affect people as they get older and has to do with an imbalance of certain proteins in the brain that can damage the brain. Dementia is a general term for *'the loss of memory, language, problem solving and other thinking abilities that are severe enough to interfere with daily life.'* (Alzheimer's Association) According to the NHS, about 850 000 people in the UK have been diagnosed with dementia, and this is one of the biggest challenges in health care.

One in three people will care for someone with dementia. Caring for someone with dementia will test you to the limit. It will take you on a surreal journey where logic has no place and where patience, kindness and compassion are essential. Dementia can be a restless place of confusion and delusion, repetition, and anxiety.

Alzheimer's disease is the most common form of dementia, but other forms we carers need to be aware of are:

- **Vascular** – caused by problems in the blood supply to the brain.

- **Lewy Body** - a progressive condition affecting movement and motor control. Hallucinations are a common symptom.

- **Frontotemporal** – a group of dementias that affect personality, behaviour, as well as language and speech.

- **Mixed dementias** – some people may develop different types of dementia, the two most common are Alzheimer's and Vascular dementia.

Although symptoms for each form of dementia may differ, most people living with dementia will experience some form of memory loss, may not recognise people or places they know, and their behaviour may become unusual and out of character, or they may act out sexually. Some people with dementia lose weight because chewing and swallowing become more difficult for them. Their speech and mobility may be affected. They may also become incontinent. Dementia is usually a slow decline, so all these symptoms could take time to manifest.

Anxiety is something that affects most people living with dementia, and as a care worker, your job will be to try to avoid any anxiety or stress to your client. How you communicate with them is key to keeping them calm and at ease. Remember that dementia affects the way people express themselves, and so it is up to *you* to learn new ways to try to understand and communicate with them. This means going along with whatever the client says or does unless it is harmful to them or others.

Because their memory is fading, a client who is living with dementia may wake up one day and demand to know who you are and what you are doing in his home. He may accuse you of stealing his possessions or trying to poison him (when administering medication). One day, you may find a client waiting anxiously at the window in the late afternoon 'waiting for the children to come home.' These could all be symptoms of dementia and you need to respond with patience and kindness.

Caring for people living with dementia

The Alzheimers.gov website[1] is a wonderful resource for information about caring for people living with Alzheimer's/ dementia. I have included some tips that have worked for me and others in the care industry.

- Routine is key in the lives of people with dementia, so try to do certain things at the same times every day – bathing, eating, dressing.

- Mealtimes should also be consistent and taken in a familiar place every time if possible, or where the client feels safe. Practicing patience is key around mealtimes as eating can be a slow affair for someone with dementia.

- Ensure that the client is dressed comfortably.

- Encourage the client to do as much as possible for herself when dressing or bathing if she is still physically able.

- Try to plan activities with the client and do them at the same time every day.

Communication

As dementia progresses, a person may not be able to process information easily, and their responses may be delayed. Often, they will stop initiating conversation, so it's up to you to make it happen. Consider these ways to help you communicate better with your client:

- Make eye contact with your client and encourage them to do the same with you.

- *Never* negate what the client is saying. They have entered a different reality to yours so it will just upset them unnecessarily.

---

[1] *https://www.alzheimers.gov/life-with-dementia/tips-caregivers*

- To keep them calm and at ease, just go along with it. Do not argue with them. Let them believe what they want to.

- Keep life simple for them by not giving them too many choices – it will only confuse them and cause them anxiety. Give them choices that elicit yes or no answers only.

- If they are not making sense, try to find the meaning behind their words (easier said than done), and always acknowledge what they have said. Never say 'you are not making sense' because for them, they are. Try to find context, assess the circumstances to get some clues.

- Give your client time to respond. Don't interrupt him. Practice patience.

- If your communication isn't working, try re-phrasing your question.

- When communicating with people with dementia, talk as you would normally to an adult (and not as to a child) *but* try to speak more slowly and more clearly, using simple language and short sentences.

- *Do not* try to test their memory by saying things like 'do you remember when…?' Or showing them photos and asking if they recognise the people or places in the pic, or asking 'do you know who I am?' This may only cause confusion and anxiety. The lesson is to just *listen* to whatever they say and go along with it.

- Do not speak about the person in company as if they are not there. Their right to dignity and respect does not disappear with dementia.

- Keep your tone of voice friendly and calm.

Communication is not just about words. One communicates through body language too – gestures, facial expressions, movement, and touch are ways to help you connect with your client. These ways of communication, are important, especially when speech is affected. When using non-verbal communication try to be calm and patient.

Be aware of your client's personal space – some people feel intimidated if someone else gets too close. If they allow it, hold their hand while talking as this helps to reassure them. Always watch their body language to gauge whether they are comfortable with that.

Remember – communication is a two-way process. It will be made easier if you:

- Actively listen to what is being communicated.

- Don't interrupt.

- Give them your full attention.

- Minimise any distraction – turn off TV, radio etc.

- Repeat what has been said and ask if that's accurate.

Just because someone has dementia does not mean they cannot live active and fulfilling lives. However, these activities would have to be initiated by others - family, friends, and care workers. Find things that stimulate the person physically, mentally, and socially, as well as creatively. These activities may need to be simplified for the person living with dementia to enjoy. Shared activities are encouraged, and the senses play a significant role in keeping a client with dementia actively living. Playing music, singing, dancing, working in the garden, walking, hand massages, and visiting beautiful places of interest are all activities you can do with your client. When out and about with your client, be mindful of their level of anxiety. Some people do not like loud noises and crowds.

We often use words that are negative (*'unbearable'*), pessimistic (*'hopeless'*) or frightening (*'tragic'*), when talking about the impact of dementia. But for some, how dementia affects them is not always negative, it can be varied. *Wendy Mitchell*, a person living with dementia and author of *One Last Thing*, and *What I wish people knew about dementia*, discovered that one can look at dementia as *'the end of one's life or the start of a different life.'* We need to be mindful of how we talk about dementia by changing our words. Dementia *is life changing, challenging and stressful* as are many aspects of most people's lives.

When interacting with someone with dementia, remember:

62

BE KIND

BE GENTLE

BE RESPECTFUL

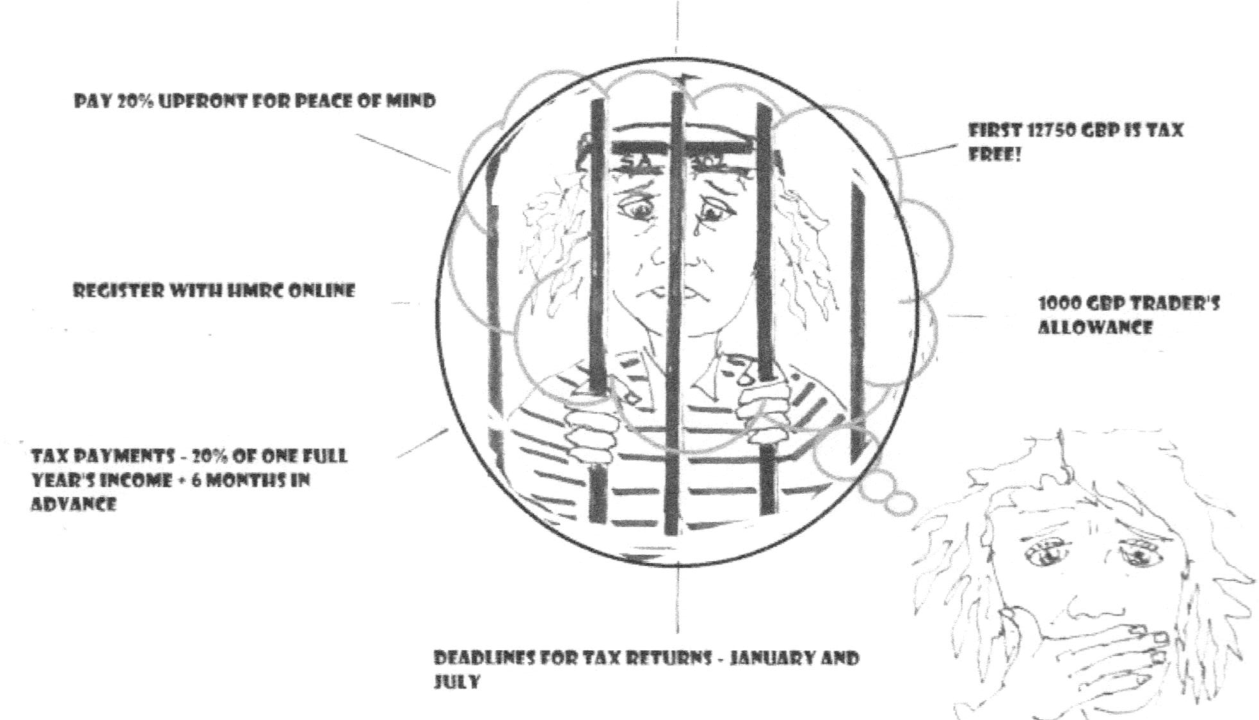

GET OUT OF JAIL FREE!
TAX YEAR - APRIL 6 TO APRIL 5
PAY 20% UPFRONT FOR PEACE OF MIND
FIRST 12750 GBP IS TAX FREE!
REGISTER WITH HMRC ONLINE
1000 GBP TRADER'S ALLOWANCE
TAX PAYMENTS - 20% OF ONE FULL YEAR'S INCOME + 6 MONTHS IN ADVANCE
DEADLINES FOR TAX RETURNS - JANUARY AND JULY

- 13 -

TAXING TIMES

UK income tax explained by Gerda Fouché

'Kindness is the language which the deaf can hear and the blind can see.' - **Mark Twain**

As a live-in carer you are obliged to register as a taxpayer with the Her Majesty's Revenue and Customs (HMRC) and submit a tax return every year. It can feel daunting having to negotiate a different tax system and you may want to seek the advice of a tax consultant. You will find professional tax consultants in most centres, or you can go online.

Fellow carer, Gerda Fouché, speaks the language of tax far better than I, and she offers a succinct outline of this tricky subject.

'I have been caring for six years in the UK. In my previous life, I had a small accounting practice and did tax returns for clients.

When I moved to the UK, I concentrated on learning new skills, which included using the public transport system, navigating the interpersonal minefield which comes with our profession, and juggling all the balls which make up our lives as carers. The last thing I wanted to learn was a new tax system – I had turned my back on that world. But after a disastrous experience with a recommended 'professional,' I decided to trust my own ability and skills once more.'

The tax system works as follows (a simplified explanation).

The UK tax year is from 6 April (2024) to 5 April of the next year (2025). Please note: the figures quoted pertain to the 2024/2025 tax year. These may change in the future.

- **Taxable income** - If you earn between £12 571 and £50 270 a year, you will *pay 20% tax on your earnings. Any earnings paid into your bank account* during this time would be the amount to declare to HMRC. If your last invoice before 5 April is only *paid* in after that date, then it would fall in the next tax year.

Your first tax return would be due (if done online) in January of the following year (2026). Tax forms become available just after the tax year closes, so they can be submitted any time after that but *before* the end of January. It may be helpful to have it done sooner rather than later.

- **Personal allowance** - The first £12 570 of your earnings is tax-free. However, you must declare your total earnings. The HMS deducts the tax-free amount in their calculations, before applying the tax and NI rates.

- **Trading allowance** - Some carers prefer to keep things simple and claim the £1000 trading allowance instead of claiming expenses. For most live-in carers, that more than covers allowable deductions. However, if you choose to submit your expenses instead, you will need invoices or printed receipts for every expense. The tax office will not accept just your bank statements as proof of expenses. Electronic invoices and receipts are also acceptable, but make sure they are backed up!

- **National insurance** - NI goes towards funding the National Health Service (NHS), pension funds and social benefits. As a self-employed taxpayer, you must pay Class 4 National Insurance, depending on your profit (amount after deductions). These amounts change every year, and you can check it on the UK government website.[1]

You must pay six months tax and NI in advance for the next year (tax return due in January). The balance for the second half of the tax year is due in July. This means in effect that when you file your tax return, it is paid for.

Every six months going forward, you will pay the advance tax based on your previous tax return earnings.

It gets a little trickier when you are *self-employed* and *employed* at the same time (you may work privately as well as for an

---

[1] *https://www.employedandselfemployed.co.uk/self-employed-tax-calculator*

agency). Your employer will issue a *P60, (or P45)* (end-of-the-year certificate issued to employees by the HMRC which summarises your earnings and tax contributions). All employed income is declared to HMRC by the employer, along with any tax deductions made. You need to declare your *total* income to HMRC, after which the tax-free portion and any expenses (or trading allowance) is applied. You are taxed on the *total of all earnings*. The SA302 form will show the total tax payable. You would then pay over the difference between the SA302 amount, and any tax deducted on your P60 or P45.

The lessons I learnt from my experience were:

- Check out your tax consultant.

- You are responsible for whatever gets filed on your behalf.

- Insist on seeing the SA302 (the statement by the HMRC giving evidence of your earnings) before the tax return gets filed and make sure you understand it.

- Pose questions to whoever files your tax for you if you do not agree with the figures.

- As a self-employed taxpayer, it is better to practice your own version of PAYE and pay the tax regularly to the HMRC – eventually you do get a bit of interest credited to your tax account, which can go towards paying the next tax bill.

- The first full year you earn a decent income as a self-employed person, but you will get the shock of your life when the first SA302 arrives. You are paying tax in arrears for a year, and half of the next year's tax in advance for 6 months,

- Any deductions claimed must be 'in the production of income.' There are specific circumstances which allow expenses to be claimed. A word of caution: don't get 'creative,' as further down the line you may be selected for an audit and it could cost you penalties and interest, or even jail time. When HMRC discovers or is informed of the errors, the penalty for 'lack of reasonable care' is between 0% and 30% of the extra tax amount due. If it is deliberate, the penalty is 20% to 70% of the extra tax amount due. If it is deliberately concealed, it is between 30% and 100% of the extra tax amount due. Depending on the scale of the offence, it may be your '*Go to Jail*' card. So, if there are mistakes, best to come clean, correct them, and plead your case. That is, unless you desire to explore the inner workings of the UK prison system.

To sum up my humble advice to any live-in carer: in order to avoid the shock of advance tax payments, make the HMRC a beneficiary with your bank, and in your first year pay over 25% of your weekly self-employed income to HMRC, using your *UTR (Unique Tax Reference number* - you receive this when you register as a taxpayer) *with a K* behind it. Thereafter, you can drop the payments to your average tax rate. If you are unsure of what it is, pay over 20%. You get a better interest rate on money paid in advance than you would at the bank! The HMRC bank account number is 12001039, sort code 083210, beneficiary is HMRC Cumbernauld.

- 14 -

ONE LAST THING...
a note on dying.

'At birth we cry. At death we understand why.'
- Bulgarian proverb

You may often hear people saying that old age is not for sissies. But neither is caring for the aged. It is not everyone's cup of tea. Many of us have heard our friends say to us,' *I don't know how you do it. I could never do what you do.*' Even clients have said such things! There are moments when things are particularly trying– and they can be – that I question myself too. One of the challenges that a carer may face is the death of a client.

Being with someone at the end of their life can be an incredibly special time – if you as a carer are prepared. When asked *'what do you consider a good death?'* people respond, *'an easy death with no suffering and my family with me,'* or similar sentiments. It can be frightening to think about our own mortality. Yet, one thing is certain, death is unavoidable. It is part of the cycle of life.

Fortunately, conversations and discussions about death are more acceptable these days. There are death cafés, and groups who discuss how to prepare for death. There are dying with dignity debates, and people who work as death doulas, helping the dying and their families through this transition. There are numerous books written on the subject, from the practical aspect to the spiritual and beyond.

Unless you choose to work in a specialised field of care, you will most likely be caring for someone who is much older than you and more than likely, has health issues. It is important to check that all information regarding next of kin and who to call in case of an emergency (ICE) are recorded and up to date in the client's care plan. Also, make sure you know where the *DNAR (Do Not Attempt Resuscitation)* form is if there is one.

Someone can die a *Natural death* or an *Unnatural death*. A natural death is when someone succumbs to a terminal illness. An unnatural death is when someone dies unexpectedly, be it from a heart attack, or a stroke, or something unknown. However, a coroner will have to be notified in the case of an unnatural death.

You may care for a client who is terminally ill and experience the gradual process of their dying. This can be an enriching experience, and you can play a meaningful role in those last weeks, days, hours, and even minutes of your client's life. It can be a gentle letting go.

However, if one day you discover your client is unresponsive and not breathing, you must act quickly. The first thing to do is *Remain Calm and Breathe*. And then spring into action.

1. Apply your first aid knowledge of ABC – open the Airways by tilting the head back, check the Breathing and if there is none, call 999. These calls can be frustrating and time-consuming if you don't have up-to-date, correct information at hand. Make sure you have the client's name, date of birth, address, and medical info to give the operator. If the client has a DNAR (Do Not Attempt Resuscitation) directive in place, give the operator this info, and follow their advice. If there is no DNAR, start CPR until the emergency services arrive.

2. If your client is old but in fairly good health, and dies unexpectedly in the night, call 999 and follow their advice. *Do not touch anything in the room*, as this is considered an 'unnatural' death.

3. Contact the client's next of kin.

Remember that every religion and culture has its own rituals, beliefs and mysteries surrounding death. Be mindful of that and give whatever relevant information there is in the care plan – your client's wishes or instructions – to the emergency services.

If your client has died and the family has been told, you also need to inform the agency you work with as soon as possible.

Some families ask the carer to stay on to keep the household going while they deal with the funeral arrangements. It is your choice whether to do so but remember that this is a time when the family will need help with all kinds of practicalities. Be helpful if you can. Just keeping the teapot full, or making a meal, can be a godsend at times like these.

When someone dies, emotions run high, and things can be said or done that are hurtful, angry, and painful.

In the words of Don Miguel Ruiz – '*Always speak with integrity. Never take anything personally. Never make assumptions. Always do your best.*' These are known as the four agreements and are invaluable in the world of caring.

WE ALL NEED A HELPING HAND IN OUR LIVES SOMETIMES

- 15 -

CONCLUSION

'Accomplishing something provides the only real satisfaction in life' - **Thomas Edison**

Like many experiences in life, care work has changed me. It has brought out the best and the worst in me. It has taught me the meaning of connection, of living every moment fully. It has taught me humility and shaped my view on life. It has also helped me hone my skills of observation and self-reliance. In my time as a care worker, I have repaired Nutri-bullets, installed washing machines, fixed vacuum cleaners, designed, and sewn specialised aids for clients, jump-started car batteries, and somehow managed to work out the controls on some strange heating systems! Oh, and of course, I have changed many a light bulb.

These are not necessarily the *duties* of a carer but doing them saved a lot of time and bother (and money for the client) and learning how to do things I'd never done before gave me a great sense of satisfaction. Challenging myself to try new things also helps me feel connected to the world beyond the four walls of a client's home. Those little accomplishments were often the sparkle in my day which lifted my spirits if I was feeling low.

But the most impressive lesson of all has been the importance of meaningful interaction and communication. Caring has given me a profound understanding of the human condition and the interconnectedness of life.

I hope this booklet has been useful to you and has offered you a deeper understanding of the life of a live-in carer. If you choose to pursue this line of work,

I wish you the best of clients, a comfortable bed to sleep in, and many new friends along the way.

 For many of you, the experience will be as much about adapting to a new country and culture as it will be about caring. You will have to navigate your way through how things work in the new country. The best route to follow is to be open to new experiences, ask a lot of questions, and make use of the internet, social media and the local library to find out as much as you can about your new world. May you travel this path with compassion, kindness, and empathy as your guides.

If life is a journey, I wish you *Güte Reise, Bon Voyage, Góða Ferð and Have a Nice Trip!*

ACKNOWLEDGEMENTS

Deep gratitude goes to my twin sister, Shelagh for all her words of encouragement and support in helping me to complete this book. She gave of her time to read, comment, and edit it - *pùsund þakkir, systir mín!* And to Lindsay Stewart, who also deftly sifted through the mire of my words, offering gems of insight and jewels of advice - a *big* thank you! Gerda Fouché - a warrior like no other, who gave wise counsel regarding tax issues and caring in general - thank you so much, baie dankie!

I'd also like to thank the many carer friends I have made, who shared their words of wisdom for this book, especially Sarah Gobey - a friend for life, Ruth Walden - self-confessed hippie and accidental travel agent, Bev Tromp - the radio head, Sue Maule - a woman of the gentlest kind, and Lynne Lotter, Louise Johnson, Astrid Bellingan, Rachel Herd, Wendy Thompson, and so many others I have chatted to about our experiences as live-in carers.

My appreciation and thanks also to those carers who set up support groups on social media so that live-in carers could have some form of community, albeit digital. These groups have proved to be an invaluable source of comfort, information, and connection. Through these platforms I have met many people and spent time with them walking in the woods, going on road trips together, and sharing our experiences - often with much hilarity. Thank you!

USEFUL LINKS AND REFERENCES

Training Online
- Training Online – https://carecoursesonline.co.uk
- Caredemy – https://caredemy.co.uk
- Careskills Academy – https://www.careskillsacademy.co.uk
- Social Care, TV – https://www.social-care.tv
- HL Online Training – https://www.hlonlinetraining.co.uk
- The Health and Safety Group – https://thehealthandsafetygroup.com

Insurance For Care Workers
- Fish Insurance – https://www.fishinsurance.co.uk
- Surewise – https://www.surewise.com
- Mark Bates Ltd – https://markbates.link/Angelsis

Useful websites
- Angels Introductory Services – www.angelsis.uk
- Live In Care Jobs – https://www.liveincarejobs.co.uk
- Carers Matter – https://carersmatter.co.uk
- Alzheimer's Society UK – https://www.alzheimers.org.uk
- Age UK – https://www.ageuk.org.uk
- Dementia UK – https://www.dementiauk.org
- NHS – https://www.nhs.uk
- UK Government Website – https://www.gov.uk
- NACAS- National Association of Carers and Support workers – https://nacas.org.uk/
- Union For Care Workers – https://careworkersunion.org
- LOVESPACE – https://lovespace.co.uk
- Send my bag – https://www.sendmybag.com

Facebook carer pages and support groups – you will need to request to join.
- Carers from any country working in the UK for Support and Companionship
- Live in Care Workers (UK)
- Care Work South Africa to UK
- Care Workers UK and RSA Affiliates and Referral Services
- Angels Home Care Introductory Service – self-employed live-in Carers' posts
- Carer's Accommodation – Long and short term.

RECOMMENDED READING

Pema Chödrön – *When Things Fall Apart – Heart Advice for Difficult Times.*

Viktor Frankel – *Man's Search for Meaning.*

Emma Healey – *Elizabeth is Missing.*

Nan Little – *If I Can Climb Mt Kilimanjaro, Why Can't I Brush My Teeth.*

Wendy Mitchell – *What I Wish People Knew About Dementia.*

Wendy Mitchell – *One Last Thing.*

Sally Magnusson– *Where Memories Go.*

Dr Michael Mosley – *Just One Thing.*

Peter Dunlap-Shohl – *My Degeneration: A Journey Through Parkinson's.*

Felicity Warner – *The Soul Midwives Handbook.*

ABOUT THE AUTHOR

FIONA SMITH has worked as a live-in carer in the UK for more than a decade. She has worked through agencies, as well as privately, and also in an exclusive care home.

She is a qualified aromatherapist and reflexologist, as well as a trained storyteller and writer. When not caring for someone, Fiona likes to facilitate storytelling workshops and to travel. Her roaming has taken her to many parts of the globe, but connection with friends and family dotted around the world remains the life spring for her well-being.

Her constant companions are Amigo - her mascot pup, a heart-shaped stone found in the Karoo, and an imaginative mind. And books.

AUTHOR'S NOTE

Thank you for reading The Live-in Carer's Handbook. I hope you enjoyed it and found it useful and insightful. I would be so grateful if you could leave a review so that others may also be encouraged to read it. You can contact me on fionaliveincare.info@gmail.com if you would like to know more about live-in care work in the UK or caring in general. You can also read more of my personal experiences as a live-in carer on my blog:

https://montanaraves.blogspot.com/

www.ingramcontent.com/pod-product-compliance
Lightning Source LLC
Chambersburg PA
CBHW051004050726
47592CB00007B/2694